ANCESTRAL WORSHIP

A Chameleon Press book

ANCESTRAL WORSHIP
ISBN 978-988-18623-8-9

Published by Chameleon Press Ltd.
15/F, 1506-7 Pacific Plaza, 418 Des Voeux Road West, Hong Kong
www.chameleonpress.com

First printing 2014

Cover photo credit: Amber Matthews

ANCESTRAL WORSHIP

poems

DAVID McKIRDY

chameleon press
hong kong

Contents

PORTRAIT GALLERY

HERE AND THERE

Also by David McKirdy

Accidental Occidental (Chameleon Press 2005, 2010)

To Michael and Betty Kadoorie,
dear friends through thick and thin

Introduction

This collection is a homage to Hong Kong, my adopted city and to my mother and father who both passed away during the writing of many of these poems. It takes as its starting point a few poems from my first collection, *Accidental Occidental*, which are included.

The first section, titled 'Ancestral Worship', begins with the title poem but thereafter is laid out more or less in chronological order starting in 1960 with the ocean journey out from Britain to Hong Kong, during which I celebrated my fourth birthday. It deals partially with the Hong Kong of my youth and my relationship with the modern-day city that I have grown up with. Some of the pieces tackle the relationship between the colonisers and the colonised in British Hong Kong during the 1960s and 70s, when it was still a colony with a capital C and inequality and unfairness was rife. Other poems tackle how attitudes and approaches changed from the late 1960s onwards, coinciding with my own teenage years and political and social awakening.

My childhood memories are of course filtered through distance and time and probably represent a blend of mythology, dreams, wishful thinking and even a smattering of truth. Over recent years I have been encouraged by the reaction to my poems, which have been thoroughly 'road-tested' at my local poetry group Outloud, as well as further afield where I had the privilege to read to an attentive audience at The Singapore National Museum in a gallery festooned with the work of Impressionist artists including Van Gogh and Degas. I also read at the thousand-year-old Temple Of Literature in Hanoi, Vietnam, where an elderly gentleman embraced and kissed me after one of my poems was read in the Vietnamese translation. Finally I read at Brown University to the Asian Students Association where I introduced the poem Ancestral Worship in English and Cantonese.

I am indebted to my publisher and good friend Peter Gordon, who had the perspicacity and courage to point out when I had let my emotion get the better of me and taken a poem or two towards the purple end of the spectrum; he also encouraged me to be more conscious and consistent with internal rhythm and rhyme as well as to be mindful of the authenticity of voices other than my own in some of the poems. In some cases, public reading has caused me to re-assess and edit the work, in others it was clear that they resonated in their original form.

* * *

I consider myself an Asian writer. Hong Kong has always been a city of immigrants and I am simply one more who has been welcomed and made the city my home. Whether you live in Hong Kong or have never visited, I hope you might find something within these pages that speaks to you.

David McKirdy
Hong Kong, April 2014

Ancestral Worship

Ancestral Worship

I've got the blood of China in my veins
not through father, mother or distant forebears
but passed on from another's ancient line.
Seven pints passed through the eye of a needle
the anonymous gift of life
for a bastard son, a white ghost!

I feel different
as I look at life
through my wider
less jaundiced eyes.

We Chinese treasure our traditions
but whose ancestors should I worship now
mine, or his?
Maybe I'll just give thanks
pay homage to an eternal Mother
and the universal Father.

Outward Bound

Hannibal crossed The Alps
for conquest and glory.
We, adventurers of a different stripe
crossed the sea
destination Hong Kong
on the P&O liner
S.S. Carthage
built by fellow Scots, launched on our own River Clyde.

Up the gangway hand in hand we boarded
working class folk with boot-strap aspirations
to cabins
second class
the apartheid of imperial caste.
No P.O.S.H. travel for us but S.O.S.O. -
'Starboard out, staying out'
unlike that great general
never coming home
to disappointment and betrayal.

As we wave goodbye streamers sever our links
leaving monochrome memories and the 1950s in our wake
through Port Said, Suez, Aden and beyond
black-and-white Britain displaced, obscured
forgotten by senses now shaken by
shocking, pungent, grating
colours, odours and sounds
familiarity growing as we travel ever Eastward
warm and wet like a return to the womb.

Perhaps I'll linger here a while.

Writing History

Chinese gentlemen in traditional robes
inhabit the streets of my youth
scribes with folding tables and chairs
inkstone and brushes
gaunt classical scholars
performing exquisite calligraphy - for utility
in the service of
illiterate labourers.
The highest expression of the literary arts
reduced to mere communication.

Letters home to be read and narrated
by others, in other streets in other cities.
Part fortune-teller, psychologist, agony-uncle
bad news censored, rendered palatable
with subtlety and nuance
good tidings enhanced.

In another place, another time
they would be
magistrates, court officials
rather than abroad in significance
at the sharp end of the historical narrative
the collective amanuensis of a country in chaos.

Citizen Ship

For Leung Ping Kwan

We arrived on the same day
you in the hold of a fishing junk
me on the ocean liner.
Settling into a three-story house
the shipping crates were delivered by noon
discarded, they made a hut for you on the hill.

We lived on either side of the same street
kept apart by the wall between
a physical and symbolic shield
to prevent disease, or 'going native'.

We tried to connect
but concrete and closed minds are tough to conquer
a barrier for inhibitions carelessly thrown
not so for hurled rocks and insults.

We flew kites across the top
swooping and dancing as one
the caress
then the cut of the string.

We learned each other's tongue
through jagged gaps
"Good morning" - "Jo San"
"How are you?" - "Nei ho ma?"
"What is your name?" - "Nei Gieu mut yeh meng?"
"Well fuck your mother!" - "Dieu nei lo mo!"

We left home together for school
you on foot
me on the bus
attending classes at either end of another street
both burdened by the hopes and expectations
of another generation.

We arrived on the same day
grew up together - apart.
One colony - two systems
two people - one future.

Star Struck

Star struck tourists
cliché their way across the harbour
in kitsch historic style
having scanned the brochures
and watched Nancy Kwan as Suzie Wong
sashay across the gangway.

But 50 years ago
Nancy Kwan as Nancy Kwan
travelled to and fro
there and back with the rest of us.
Downstairs for the unwashed masses
delivery bicycles with baskets of live chickens
British schoolboys
with long hair and a twenty-a-day habit
upstairs in first for the rest.

A burnished brass plaque declares:
'Hull built and machinery installed by
The Hong Kong and Whampoa Dock Company.'
My father built these vessels.
Northern Star, Night Star, Day Star
each one contains his essence
Shining Star, Twinkling Star
paid our school fees
Morning Star, Silver Star
put food on the table.

A Hong Kong icon
founded by Parsee merchants
designed by British shipwrights
built and crewed by Chinese working men.
The short trip between Island and Mainland
once a lifeline
now the tee-shirt experience
of a package tour
in our world city.

So government pragmatists moved the pier
surprised by a riot of protest -
the ghostly reminder
of bloodlines drawn in sand
the collective memory of a city divided
by race, ideology and fortune.

For years
governments have failed to listen.

It's our city
our heritage
our history.

Listen now.

Amah

Nanny, Auntie, Sister, Servant
a simple woman in black and white
not young, no threat
a mouth full of gold -
a gilt edged hedge against
famine, war and pestilence.

Poor and illiterate, ideal for scrubbing
but entrusted with a stranger's child
a necessity or a convenience for those
too busy, too ill, too worldly.
Trusting eternal motherly love
of any woman, for any child.
Leaving her own family deprived
of appropriate maternal attention.

Myths of hungry ghosts
one-armed swordsmen
culinary treats and Chinese opera
we absorb, acquire, adopt
an alien culture
and another mother tongue.
These bonds can never be broken -
love is thicker than blood.

Ah May, Amah, Mama
fifty years on
the shadow of your presence remains
as the wax from the candle I light for you
rolls down

like tears.

My Old Man

Old man of the street
outside, on the margins
another waste product of our society
no longer in it, but undeniably of it.
You exist amidst parked cars
with your bric-a-brac fortune; discarded shards of other's lives.
Your whole world lies in two cardboard cartons and a plastic pail
piled high and pushed on a broken-wheeled barrow.

You spend your days sleeping, watching
and smoking dog-eared dog-ends.
Never begging
but accepting any largesse that comes your way.
I never see anyone talk to you, converse with you
except for me, but I talk to babies, dogs and trees!
"Uncle have you eaten yet?
Here's a twenty for morning tea."

You're old enough to be my father
old enough to be many fathers.
What wisdom lies lost
beyond those sparkling eyes
and lopsided toothless smile?
You epitomize the ultimate end game of life
showing kindness to you
is showing kindness to our future selves.

We Chinese

In Strasbourg, three Chinese asked for directions -

in French.

I answered -

in Cantonese.

Surprised -

they tried German.

Finally -

we expressed our pleasure
at meeting fellow countrymen abroad -

in English.

Amah Rock – Mong Fu Shek

For countless festivals and tides
I have watched and waited
for my husband's return.
Now as I gaze down the valley
a change has come over our land
the village and shoreline gone in an evil upheaval
water turned to land.
Dark forms rise up as far as the eye can see
like great ships planted in the earth
draped in covers like nets.
The light of the black sky inhabits these nets
lit, as for night-fishing
by a mighty demon
trawling for souls.

Perhaps by stealing the giant sea-serpent's pearls
we have broken our pact with the sea.
Gracious goddess Tin Hau
who turned me and your son
to stone
for love and loyalty
she has forsaken us.
Noise, smoke and burning rains blow here
as barbarians race the sacred dragons
on the remains of the harbour.

I stand witness to the changes
and pray that you my love
may ever have full nets and a gentle wind
and never return to this place.

Empirical Truth

Average women from all over Britain
followed their husbands abroad.
Unremarkable, common-or-garden housewives
from council estates with communal toilets
food, fuel and opportunities limited.

Shipped out from Portsmouth by the pound
boarding with a clean sheet
the metamorphosis began.
A tacit re-education from ladies
with a tour or two of the colonies under their belts
colluding, propagating and rewriting their history.

It's a long way by steamship
from the steam laundry
to gin and gin rummy
each day another coating
of the thin veneer
of culture and constitution
for the role ahead.

Weeks later
bewildered husbands met
reconfigured, unrecognisable wives
with a new accent
new demeanor
the past - passed.

Upward mobility is easy when any way is up
and only natives below
natives with three thousand years of culture
traveling
in the opposite direction
to resettlement estates with communal toilets
food, fuel and opportunities limited.

As wind, water and fate
reshuffle the cards.

Culture Club

The Chinese opera came to town
on the back of a fleet of trucks
bouncing and crackling with bamboo and tin sheet.
A temporary cavernous corrugated cathedral
hand-built and rough-clad in shimmering layers
of razor thin steel.
The aerialist constructors, shirtless, wiry, fearless
built their theatre in six days
on the seventh day they rested
and the villagers took over.

Room for two thousand cultured souls sitting
double for standing and shoving and eating
and spitting and hanging from rafters.
Row upon row of identical elderly floral-print ladies
with jangling jade bracelets and bad perms
unaccompanied by the old men busy keeping council at the back
tobacco-coloured with strong broad faces and squat solid bodies
moulded by years of toil at ropes and nets-
a life of illiterate wisdom, another gift
from the bountiful sea.

The heady humid air, saturated
with eye-watering smells of fried spicy squid, sandalwood
Tiger Balm and other assorted herbal unguents
wafts languidly in torpid puffs and layers
as if from a priestly censer.

A deafening cacophony of laughter, cackling, cooing
and general din echoes off the roof and rises
to a crescendo as the blood-red curtains part.
The racket continues unabated
reinforced by the crash of cymbals and falling-gongs
and the cutting ostinatos of iron-wood blocks.
Strident nasal voices vie with the whole to be heard
above the vociferous accompaniment from the floor
on toy drums, bottles and furniture
and the passing over seat backs of children food and drink.

The curtains close to no acclaim
just a lengthening of the queues
for toilets food and souvenirs
and popping out to feed the meter
or another can of beer.

Curtains open and curtains close all to no avail.
Then in a pivotal scene of love, death and redemption
the crowd finally falls deathly silent and becomes an audience.
Some look sad and some sing along
with kings and courtesans, heroes and heroines.
Then spontaneous applause, standing, cheering
and a race for the exits and cars
still two scenes left but they've seen what they want.
Only women with kids and those who love song wait till the end
then slowly walk home through the night.

The stars of the show have left the stage
to return to the theatre of life.
In the stark white glare of hundred-watt bulbs
the magic has taken flight
replaced by carnage and signs of anarchy;
broken chairs, fruit rinds
and prawn heads squashed underfoot.

If you bring culture to the people
they take what they want and leave their debris
but they came and it's their culture too.

A Portrait by the Artist of a Young Man

Framed faces -
portraits from afar -
stare back at me
through photographers' windows.
Fathers, sons and brothers
family members separated
by man-made obstacles
of borders and ideology.
Reunited by the painterly skill
of an artist's hand.
The ideal family reunion
no scheduling issues
jealousies or rows.
A young man dressed his best
stands proud in black and white
his family by his side
while six hundred miles North
his alter-ego
toils by the banks of the Yangtze River.

A Red Guitar, Three Chords and the Truth

Jesus wants me for a sunbeam
or so I'm told
by guitar slingers on Sunday in the city
fanatical, evangelical, Filippinacal
with Fender Stratocasters and Marshall stacks.
Each group
more provocative than the next
louder than the Rolling Stones
but no sympathy for The Devil.
Jezebels with decibels
courting cash, canvassing for Christ.

In the cosseted comfort of the Mandarin Hotel
disgruntled guests get a rude awakening -

The call to prayer.

Speak Chinese

I speak Chinese badly, very well.
Perfectly fluent
for seven minutes
preambles of place of birth
how long in Hong Kong
how much per month
are easy
plus, you're already half way there
when every other word is "fuck"
but when talk turns to serious matters
Philosophy, abstract notions, horse racing
things get tricky.
Political nuance is a nuisance
and poor pronunciation provokes a gasp
or a chuckle
when raising a tone
might lower the tone.

Language lessons in adolescence
from delinquent chums
have stood in good stead
for simple chat or clichéd jokes
with taxi drivers, street hawkers
fish wives and shoe shiners
real people
real Hong Kong.

Chemistry

An apothecary passed me on a path
on the way to his pharmacy amongst the trees
carrying his sack and secateurs
searching out roots, herbs and funguses.

I expected Kung Fu clothes
but he was dressed like me.
Just an ordinary guy
with two kids and a mortgage
but with generations of knowledge
passed on, assimilated
absorbing the harmony of wind and water
soothing, calming
against the ever encroaching clamour
of vertical living
and anonymous lift-shaft thoroughfares

With modernity and tradition in transition
the earth spins on
and continues to provide.

Ambushed

An elderly man approached
asking about a toilet for his wife
such a lovely old lady
how could I leave her in distress?
"Come Auntie
you're welcome to use my home."

As I turned, one became two
Two became five and finally nine
all queued up and smiling
with me handing out soap and towels
like a washroom attendant in a massage parlour
then the questioning began.

No one expects the Chinese inquisition!
Forget name, rank and serial number
these are no mere amateurs
Cantonese aunties are better
than The KGB at getting results.
Name
age, place of birth
do I own, or rent
how much per month
married, how many children?
I could have stood a beating
but they were much too subtle for that
calling me by name and talking in turn.
I managed to hang on to my one testicle
and annual salary
but only because their bus was leaving.

But they know where I live
and they'll be back!

Incensed

Holy banyans
fragrant camphor and sandalwood
venerable ancient living things
torn from hallowed ground
in Fung Shui groves
outside abandoned villages
abducted, dismembered and trussed
slaved and hooded
commodified and prostituted
by mainland tree smugglers.

Hong Kong got it's name
from the trade in sweet incense
joss sticks burned in temples a thousand leagues North.
Now money talks and tradition is carted away
parked row on row, like second hand cars
awaiting some lucky new owner
who can't see the woods for the trees.

Bamboozled

The bamboo grove outside my bedroom clicks and clacks
a living breathing wind-chime
that whistles and whispers
the secrets of lives governed by seasons
unchanged for generations.

Hakka wanderers brought by the wind
came here
seduced to stay
by the sheltered cove
sweet fresh water
and these same soporific sounds.

I was the first foreigner for years
now we outnumber the villagers
and vote for each other at election time
neo-colonialists
seeking to civilise, educate
stop the building
stop the fishing
improve the marine ecology.

I voted for
Mr. Yeung Tin San
a Hakka elder
a realist who values tradition.
He was elected with a majority of one.

Sometimes I feel
the wind brought me here.

Working Class God

Across the nautical miles
on an island of fishermen
by the sheltered narrows of the China Sea
sits a house of God.
Built by the father's fathers of today's tillers of the waves
this temple is listed by the antiquities and monuments office
as a cultural icon of benefit to tourism
and scheduled for cleaning, re-tiling and restoration.
But it's listed as a part of life by these simple, honest folk
and scheduled for re-dedication and blessing.
For this is no Medici palace for an elegant effete and cultured deity
this is the home of a working class God with work to be done
controlling the elements, protecting the nets
and holding all vessels in a warm embrace.
Government bureaucrats, feathering their caps
want to preserve for posterity
the muted patinated tints and quaint dingy dank corners.
The villagers want a new brush to sweep clean
and paint in bright, lively, vibrant hues
of gaudily gold, red and green.
This house is not for a redundant God of antiquity
this God requires daily sustenance, libations and offerings.
He is part of the clan and everywhere visible;
in the sparkling of infinite pin pricks of light
as a gentle rain dapples the calm green sea
and deep amongst the ancient banyans
those sentinels with twisted limbs entwined in a sensual embrace
gnarled boughs that mirror the stooped backs of ancient mariners
themselves as hard and weathered as aged teak.

Now foreigners have come to Kau Sai Chau
Italians, offering their skills with open hands
that carry the genetic legacy
of Leonardo, Michelangelo, Botticelli, Caravaggio.
They delve with care amidst the treasures
and peel away the secrets of the years.
Uncovered scripts and ancient colours
reveal the hand of venerated generations
those long gone but ever present in nooks and crannies
in ancestral tablets and in the faces of boys at play.
The job is done, outsiders gone
life returns to the slow rhythmic pulse of the sea
and God rests his feet in front of the fire
at home with a cup of tea.

Abroad in England

Descend the steps and taste the air
home from exile
arrived at last in Blake's green and pleasant land.
Through Sloane Square, Westminster, Marble Arch and Holborn
conveyed underground through history
in the quiet company of undistinguished fellow travelers.
Rich man, poor man, beggar man, thief
journey in insular isolation.
The only sound the attack of wheels on rails
and the self-conscious turning to page three.

Where's the spirit that held the world at its' feet?
It kicks a ball now
colonized by mediocrity, xenophobia, tattooed housewives
and the deification of the lout and the under-achiever.

But still a nation of shopkeepers
Asians mainly
vending micro-wave meals, football, tits and beer
the latest opiates for the masses.
A weekly bath, but soap every night on TV depicts
lives more mundane than their own
played by graduates from RADA with cockney elocution.
"Alas poor Yorick, wot a prat."
Dross dressed as entertainment, masquerading as art.
exciting inanity, mundane urbanity.

No sign of Jeeves and Wooster, or genteel decay
or cricket on village greens
or scholarly gents in trilby hats
or courtesy, efficiency, or care.

I came to find my centre and see my place of birth
an ideological-We won the bloody war-Englishman
visiting a post-war, post-empire, post-punk outpost
to confirm some utopian vision and the lies propagated in school.
A madness fostered by too much distance and too much time
masked my total alienation from this totally alien nation.
So I'll return cynically, clinically wiser
an accidental occidental, re-oriented
to where my homely heart is
East of Suez.
Far East and away.

'Where the hills and streams end
there seems no road beyond
amidst the shady willows
and bright flowers
one more village (Yau Yat Chuen)' — Lu Yu

Fragrant Harbour

From the summit of Flying Goose Mountain
survey the realm of the Nine Dragons - Kowloon
a linguistic anomaly, transliterated into a word
devoid of the meaning and mythology
of this ring of eight mountains
each inhabited
by the spirit of a mighty beast
ruled by the Sung Emperor
ensuring peace and prosperity
for those
living within this gaze.

Two cities one location
two linguistic narrative arcs
of our history
each name in Cantonese
a sign post for what went before
a route-guide to the past
a palimpsest of urban overlay
and blade-runner shards
Nike and Reebok's
plus-size commercial footprint
obscuring
Yau Ma Tei - 'oil and sesame fields'
now concrete high-rise.
Sham Shui Po - 'deep water pier'
miles from the sea.
Hung Hom - 'red cliff'
as flat as a plain.
Yau Yat Chuen - 'one more village'
a bucolic poetic concept amidst dense city-scape.

We live in a magical land, unseen, unheeded
masked by busy blinkered lives.
Underfoot the bedrock and foundation of our city remains
ghosts of knife-sharpeners, letter-writers
rickshaw coolies, sampan girls.
The faint footfalls of those gone before.
What will we leave
as we sink into the past?

Return of the Queen

The QE2 came home to The Clyde
like a salmon returning to spawn.
She berthed at Greenock's wharf
to a festive expression of pride
that Scotland's finest flowers
in steam and ships and men
had departed from these shores.
Tied fast she strained at the leash
standards festooned from stern to bow
from ship to shore and beyond
wind-blown like Tibetan prayers.

I too returned this year
a prodigal pilgrimage.
No one lined the quay
for my arrival
but my shadow
paced the well-worn path.
I could have been a riveter
a welder, a shipbuilder -
the Brahmins of the industrial age
I would have had a hand
in the making

read the obituary
at the end.

But another destiny awaited me -
we also departed, running
unclear if it was towards, or from, something
perhaps both
a Hajj and Hejira combined.

Now like the big ships
I'm all at sea in my native land
constantly drawn to that foreign field

made home.

Dying Flowers

For my father

Arriving from the plane to an empty home
I notice the garden, untended, forlorn
in the back dandelions and flowers both
brown and dying
from weed-killer indiscreetly strewn
by fingers less green than yours.

Last year I fixed the fence
cobbled together
with scraps of wood and two-inch nails.
It might last a year
"That's long enough," you said.

The year before she died
I drove you both
over high-roads and by-roads
old haunts
walked years ago hand-in-hand.
In the back seat
you, by then lame and blind
opened the window
sniffed at the memories
and gulped cold polo-mint air.
Hand-in-hand
you chattered like children
on a day-trip from school.

Later I bathed you
as you did me in infancy
a filial debt finally repaid.

Alone, your care in other's hands
I, now an outsider, trimmed your moustache
held your hand and listened
as you joked and sang some favourite songs.

The day you died
the wind-damaged fence lost a board
and your flowers gave up the fight.

Corporate Identity

In Sai Kung Town
gambling grannies congregate
in The Ronald Room
with rows of gold teeth flashing
beneath the golden arches.
The baby-sat run riot
as septuagenarian sitters
preoccupied, pass on tips and loans
discuss runners and riders
odds and options.
A real life Joy-Luck Club
win lose or draw
"They're lovin' it".

Shining

Mr. Lee the shoe-shine boy
is a proud man
still working at 82
still paying his way.
He'll shine my shoes for free
because I give him 'face'
calling him 'Uncle'
conversing, showing respect.

We're both immigrants
he from Indonesia
me from Scotland.
His generation made Hong Kong
today his clients read a paper
send a text
or gaze mutely at the top of his head.
He says I see into his heart
"Sir, what's your name?" he asks
"Chiu Chow Gum" I reply.
This is a euphemism for
crater-faced son of a bitch!
"That's a fine name" he says,
"No one will forget you."

I accept the gift of shiny shoes
and reciprocate with tea-money.
He claims to be the finest shiner in Hong Kong
he's certainly the best psychologist
I pay fifty bucks over the odds
and leave a happy man.

Homecoming

Flying home from the land of my birth
rituals performed, eulogy delivered
orphaned and pensive.
A little Chinese boy sleeps
with his head on my knee
trusting and innocent
I slide my pillow under him
and spread a blanket
as his mother snores beside him.
Later we chat
"Uncle, are you a foreigner?"
"Yes, born in Scotland."
"Why can you speak Cantonese?"
"I am a Hong Kong man now."
"How old are you?"
"55, and you?"
"I am 5 years old."
Just a year older than me
when I left
traveling towards a new life.
50 years absence has made me
a venerable uncle
with an inscrutable Western smile
heading back to my Chinese home.

PORTRAIT GALLERY

Why

For Teo d'Auriol

What purpose does this loss serve
in what grand scheme could this ever be right?
A little boy just twelve years old
invested with faith and expectation
our message in a bottle
lovingly placed in the river of life
dashed on the rocks on the way to the sea.

The vessel lies broken but the spirit endures
touching those he never met.
Now lighter than air, floating dancing in eddies
dipping a wing, caressing the source
to produce infinite concentric circles
intersecting those made by tears
painting a pattern of love for all time.

Friends for a Day

For Simon Powell

We met through your wife
and mine
two Indian painters
at home abroad
too much in common
including us.

Kindred spirit twins
sharing chemo cocktails
in two rooms
at the edge of other worlds
the only doppelganger clanger
our different physiology.

Poetry, cancer, classic bikes
too much that binds.
We met for a day
in your London club
sinking into leather chairs
as deep as a rich man's wallet.
I felt like Phileas Fogg
before departing back East.
With virtual-epistles and photos
we agreed to meet in my world
and ride bikes for a day
but...

My spare Norton still waits
fueled up and ready to roll
I'll ride it this week
in your stead
a vicarious valediction

but "last one to the top is a sissy!"
is no fun as one.

We were friends for a day
friends enough for life.

Grace Under Fire

For Muriel, The Lady Kadoorie

My dear friend Muriel is 93
she speaks English, French and Cantonese
often all at the same time
utterly unintelligible
to those unwilling to listen
with their hearts
as well as their ears
but a bit of patience goes a long way
and holding hands is good.

She recites prayers in Hebrew
and long in the past
Japanese was a possibility
but being a lady
she refused to converse
with those impolite enough
to lock her up for four years
surrounding her family
with guns and barbed wire.

Spoken words and their absence resonate
fluent in some
mute in others
a linguistic road map of a lifetime
of dignity and grace under fire
and rain
sunshine
and stardust.

Time spent in her presence
a blessing
a vicarious duty and a pleasure
in the stead of my own mother and father
six thousand miles absent.

Rainbow

For Patrick Lieberman

Picture the rainbow
a shock of colour
a slash of hope
shot through a moment in time.

The lightest smiling touch
of an effervescent Peter Pan
with a lust for life
jauntily and lightly worn.

A message of gratitude
for the gift of passion
and flowers placed finally
in the quiet grasp of a loving hand.

The same strong, soft, creative hand
that wrote and spoke with colour
and held you under African skies.
That boundless heart that holds you still.

Blessed

For Niki Gould

Turn on the TV, open a book
everywhere you look there's a God
but where was he in your hour of need
busy on some televangelist's talk show?
Payment for prayer the business at hand
but every night you count the cost.

But each new day you count your blessings
the glorious gift of a life
entrusted to your care.
A gift mitigated by special needs
and the challenge to pull through.
Is your love enough to silence the doubters?
Those who cannot see the light inside
which would blind them if set free.

Your child of Nature, of silent wisdom
who connects with open heart
and communes through chuckles, smiles and eyes
not words or hints or lies.
An innocent envoy of something holy
uncontrived, untainted love.

Epistle to Juan

For Juan Tamayo

We all lost something this day
Husband, Father, Coo Coo, Friend.
Compact, strong, independent, proud
I've seen a photo of you
as the younger man I never met
standing with your bride
movie-star handsome
sharp as a knife
cigarette in hand
smoking
Bogart-cool
on hot Havana nights.

You were gone in an instant
vibrant till your final day.
Not for you the slow decline of twilight years
you went out like the brightest of lights
your silhouette left burning on our retinas
as we look homeward, out beyond the sea you loved.

At the counting of blessing
We all gained something this day.

Song of Life

For Betty Kadoorie

Some take health for granted
not us, we've been too close
to the other side
twinned souls in sickness and in health.

Amid vines fragile roses grow
to monitor the grapes.
You're my rose
my canary in a coal-mine.
So get well, keep well
many songs remain unsung.

I write the poems
you plot a steady course.

As long as you can fly
I can sing.

Bald

Being bald is beautiful, when it exposes hidden charms
adversity, nobility, innate qualities on show
drawing out the best in those who hold each other dear
the focal point of love and good intentions.

Being bald is trendy, designer stubble for the crown
the golden dome with saffron robe, never out of style
against the fads of fashion, this week blonde, next week brown
no pretence nor defence just naked honesty.

Being bald is brave, representing pain and fear
raw courage in the face of fresh priorities
social obligations and heartfelt expectations
unimportant in the new reality.

Being bald is beautiful in the eyes of those we touch
effective inspiration affecting those who understand
the warm cocoon of home and hearth, a haven for the soul
the resonance of healing hopes, the touch of healing hands.

Digging Heaney

Between my finger and my thumb
the camera rests
poised for posterity.

Up on the stage
the saintly silver halo
pauses, priest-like
behind the rostrum
then rips a poem off the page
and slaps it into life
like a recalcitrant baby at birthing.

Three hundred fertile minds
finally hear the verse
that all had read
a dozen times.
By God, the great man can handle a stanza
deliver a poem
like you'd drive a stolen car.

Riding on waves of adolescent adulation
he paints with words
agrarian landscapes and homely hearths
a world view, condensed in one loamy sod.
The master at work
passing on, preserving
an ancient oral tradition.

Between my finger and my thumb
the camera rests

Seamus! Smile.

Gilles Villanelle

The Ferrari Tifosi chant 'Forza Italia.'
They had a new idol with Gilles Villeneuve
They deify drivers with steel genitalia.

No emotional baggage or paraphernalia
just sublime car control and sheer verve
The Ferrari Tifosi chant 'Forza Italia.'

He wanted to please all the fans, *inter alia*
the races he won were superb
They deify drivers with steel genitalia.

The risks that he took were complete braggadocia
as anyone there could observe
The Ferrari Tifosi chant 'Forza Italia.'

Gilles met his demise causing mass melancholia
the tragedy touching a nerve
They deify drivers with steel genitalia.

Gilles is long gone, but there's still memorabilia
and world champion Jacques Villeneuve
The Ferrari Tifosi chant 'Forza Italia.'
They deify drivers with steel genitalia.

HERE AND THERE

Regime Change

November 2008

In the wreck of the golden-age
a generation waits for God
and votes and hopes
for another brand new deal.

The world holds it's breath - turning blue
as Joe-Public ticks the box
a choice affecting us all -
Neo-con or simply 'Neo'?
The One.

A black man in The White House
a precedent for president.
The new messiah, or the anti-Christ?
Perhaps just another pinball wizard
finger on the button
such a supple wrist.

We all hope a cog has turned
the wake up call for the American dream.
We all have a dream:

"Free at last, free at last."

Here Be Dragons

For Nguyen Phan Que Mai

In Ha Long - 'Descending Dragon'
the spirit of that mythical mystical beast
inhabits the earth, sea and sky
repelling invaders
welcoming others with an open heart.

In Ha Long
I felt at home
having grown up
under the shadow and protection
of Hong Kong's own Nine Dragons -
'Gau Lung' District.

In Ha Long
some dragon essence entered
giving me a fever
and my words wings.

In Ha Long
I read in English
to polite applause.
The Vietnamese translation
elicited cheers, hugs and kisses
from octogenarian warrior poets
whose own verse
redolent with love and loss
declaimed in dignified dedication
pricked the heart
to flow tears of blood.

In Ha Long
Vietnam veterans from the other side
men and women both
honoured, venerated, feted.

In Ha Long
Here be dragons.

Tour de Force

2003

We've all been inspired by a man on a bicycle
those of us with our own mountain to climb.
Brave Sir Lancelot slew a dragon for us all
he came though from incredible odds
and won the second hardest race in the world.
The first was getting back on his feet
and starting over from less than square-one
it was a team effort, just like all of life
and death and survival
if he can do it so can I
we're under starter's orders.

On your bike!

Tour de Farce

2013

'It's not about the bike'
the wheels came off that some time ago
gone with the rock-star girlfriend
team mates, friends and family
all burned on your way up the mountain
by potions, persuasion and perjury
from chemical cocktails
to champagne on the Champs-Elysees.
Now you are burned in effigy
seven yellow jerseys
seven deadly sins
each one a lie.

I had your cancer
Your yellow wristband
read your book.
You were right
'It's not about the bike'.

Charlie Don't Surf

You say - Charlie he don't surf
and he don't play Rock-n-Roll
but Charlie rules the night
and he extracts a toll.

For Charlie is your lover
and Charlie is your foe
and Charlie fights and Charlie dies
until you have to go.

Charlie don't play baseball
and she don't bake apple pie
but Charlie is your darling
when it's your turn to die.

Charlie is a farmer
a father, mother too
a waitress, baker, teacher, nurse
a warrior poet true.

Charlie doesn't have the bomb
except the ones you gave
but Charlie's children feel the burn
of Napalm's fiery wave.

Charlie doesn't play banjo
or sing no country songs
but Charlie fights for freedom
in the name of Viet Cong

Charlie is your enemy
but your country makes you pay
and only Charlie understands
when you go home to stay.

The things you've seen, the hurt you feel
fill Charlie's nightmares too
for Charlie is your comrade
sharing all you've both been through.

Charlie opens up his arms
when you return to 'Nam'
to try to exorcise your ghosts
for serving Uncle Sam.

Victor Charlie is the name
Charlie, victor in this game
but Charlie doesn't crow or gloat
gets on with life, forgets the pain.

Charlie served his nation well
now he's building something more
Vietnam is just a country
no more a bloody war.

50 to 1

For Kellan Osborne

One of my friends turned 50
the day his son was born.
A new life linked by blood
and genes and the half century
that both separates and unites them.

Will he be too old to connect
in later years?
Why not connect now
and on into the future
continue to enjoy him in the present
as those future presents come to pass.

The future is what you make happen
by the actions you take now.

Evolution

Written with the students of the Swire Poemography program, 2009

If a man should fall from grace in the city
would the drop resound
or fall like a silent leaf
landing on a mirrored pond
then rise on bright white wings?
Would I be the one to take his place?

If I should fall from grace in the city
would my words rebound
from the mirrored wall
red with revolution, love and lust
redolent with lots of lovely layers of alliteration?
Would you be the one to take my place?

If you should fall from grace in the city
would you make a sound
from Asia to Atlantis
adding to the hum of the world?
Would your poems inspire?
Who would be the one to take your place?

If we should fall from grace in the city
would it be profound
would others pick up and carry the torch
as our verse speaks back from afar?
Cities come and cities go
but others remain to take our place.

For now...

Cattle Class

I've just made friends with a cow
it's tricky at first
but then the trust builds.
I feel like a cattle-egret
the job doesn't pay much
but it's honest work.
I'm in charge of stroking noses
scratching backs
and uttering sweet banalities
not so different from most day-jobs.

A nine hundred pound companion
who farts for a living inspires civility
a two-legged new best friend however
can do more damage than stampeding bulls
once the frisson of freshness has faded.
At the first signs, slowly back away
don't slip, talk too loud or wear red
then run, run like hell, climb a tree
there are always more to take your place
as in Pamplona.

Subject

My mate's making a movie about me

a documentary about those who call home, abroad
their finicky foibles, entrenched ideas and odd behaviour patterns.
I wonder how he came to the conclusion
that I was a subject worthy of treatment?
My life condensed through a lens, extracted, abstracted
coloured and filtered through prisms and glass
cropped and contorted to fit in a frame.

With yet more quirky angles to sustain interest
I - forewarned - act out my fantasies for posterity
snippets of routine falsified by ego-driven acts and omissions.
Sometimes I catch him filming and try to look cool
but it's hard to appear erudite and urbane
when there's food stuck in your teeth
or your sphincter's itching like buggery.

I wonder if he'll be kind with the cutting
capture my good side (whichever that may be)
not dwell on my bald patch and other failings?
This poses the question -
What will this voyeuristic video testament say
and are other's vicarious visions a valid endorsement?
What do people think of me anyway
and does it matter?

After all I'm not even sure what I think of me!

Word Picture

A picture is worth a thousand words
well if you've got the canvas I've got the works
but do they inspire
grab you by the throat
and shake you
or are we merely stroking egos?
It's a selfless thing
to give birth to another's conception.
How will the issue please us both
will I see my hand in what you render
can a common vision ever be?
If we both agree
please paint a picture of my words
then we'll see.

Senior Citizen

I've been to some funerals lately;
a teacher or two
friends and relatives.
My mother, my father.

They smile and thumb their noses
as they pass on the burden
and quietly slip off to another place
of timeless tenure.

We consulted our elders and betters
now, I'm an elder and better
for better or worse
but no consultations so far.

What will I say, what will I do
will wisdom emerge,
or elude me?

As my time rushes on
like the wind from the North.

Seismic Shift

2010

Neruda declared
"Déjame un subterraneo, un laberinto."
Leave me an underground haven, a labyrinth.
For 69 days, 33 of his countrymen endured
in the belly of the earth, like Jonah in the whale
supported by faith, hope and the prayers of a nation
before redemption and the ascent to the light.

This year of seismic shifts
many perished
but now the earth gives up her hostages into a new dawn.

Something miraculous occurred at Camp Hope
in the absence of uniforms, threats and guns
these 'disappeared' returned
embraced by presidents and paupers
family and foreigners.

A catharsis for Chile
wives and mothers
dignified enduring women
dance alone no more.

In Hong Kong, Dreaming of Cairo

2005

We came to Cairo to see her treasures
and saw the people.
Forget the pyramids
the real jewels are among those
whose forbears built them.

Encountering beggars cheats and robbers
we felt right at home
having contributed an additional
eleven Bohemian rogues to their numbers.

In the chaos of Cairo's
persistent perpetual anarchy
a few prodigal poems -
my offspring -
escaped in a lady's bag.
I hope they find their way
to safety
to the heart of the city
to be adopted and absorbed
like so many through time
from Nubia, Greece, Rome
Arabia, Turkey, France
now Hong Kong.

Louche decadent Cairo
nobody gets out of here untouched
and the echo of the muezzin's call
will forever draw me back
pulling like a persistent child.

Plus ça change

For Mathias Doutreleau

We are off to an inauspicious start
sharing a waiting room with 150 attendees
from a suicide bombers' convention
however they depart for Tashkent
and we board for Vientiane.
Relief turns to concern as the pilot kicks the tyres
like a neophyte car buyer.
Pre-flight check done!

Upon arrival we kiss the ground
and head to the nearest temple
in search of saffron sagacity
and retrospective blessings -
sacred string for spiritual safety.

At Vang Vieng on the road North
we feast on glutinous rice
and admire the well turned ankles
and gluteus maxima
of elegant creatures on bicycles
faces as serene and impassive
as the ancient statues that dot the landscape.
In the face of such provocative perfection
my French friend and I -
enchanted as so many before -
vow to return.
Indochine - 'plus ça change' etc.

Crossing holy rivers
we placate each naga
with offerings of candy hurled into the torrent.
As we drive deeper into the heartland
layered wood smoke drifts across a timeless horizon
under the rapidly closing red eyelids of dusk.

At Luang Namtha we spend a restless night on the floor
of a travelers-rest cum whorehouse
the following day there's bath-salts and marble
as we wallow in five star comfort in Luang Prabang.

Returning South
a leisurely fuel stop becomes a hasty retreat
as optimistic fatalists barbecue chicken
in an open fire on the gas station forecourt.
We are stopped at police checkpoints
and searched for contraband
but we're only smuggling ideas and dreams
and they slip through the net.

At journey's end we cross the Mekong one last time
into Thailand
looking forward, looking back

somehow changed.

Acknowledgements

I owe thanks to many people for support and inspiration during the writing of these poems. Thank you to:

Professor Anthony Chan, Professor Shekhur Kumta, Professor Sidney Yip and all of the staff at The Prince Of Wales Hospital, Kathleen Ahrens, Martin Alexander, Lyn Austin, Paul Balaam, Andy Barker, Professor John Carey, Ian Rosales Casocot, Amar and Mamta Chhatwal, Benny Chia, Kieron and Karen Combes, Claudio and Claire de Bedin, Sally Dellow, Morris Dirkin, Shirley Dirkin, Mathias Doutreleau, Toby Emmet, Greg and Jackie England, Marjorie Evasco, Hamish Ewart, Mark Godfrey, Peter and Elaine Gordon, Wilma and Jim Gorman, Meena and Ulrich Heinz, Louise Ho, Tammy Ho, Mike Ingham, Michael and Betty Kadoorie, Natalie, Betina and Phillip Kadoorie, Raymond Kwong, Susan Lara, Cat Lau, Christopher Lavender, Alison Lee, Leung Kwai Chung, Leung Ping Kwan, James Lewis, Beth McKirdy-Joyce, Grant Mcleman, Amber Matthews, Celia Mitchell, Sheila and Andy Mumford, Nguyen Phan Que Mai, Phillip O'Mullan, David Osborne, Martin Oxley, Alvin Pang, Melanie Ryan, Catriona Ryan-Vargas, Michael and Markie Ross, Eleanor Sacket, Helen Smith, The Reverend Alan Sorensen, Deepa Swaminathan, Prem Narain Srivastava, Tony and Elaine Sunman, Dr. Benny Tong Ying Kau, Sarah Toogood, Adrian Turner, Susan Turner, Ricardo de Ungria, Simon Valance, Xu Xi, Krip Yuson, Najam Zaidi, my mother and father, family and friends from Kowloon Docks and Gauri Narain.

Some of the poems in this collection have previously been published in *The Asian Literary Review*, Vol. 13 Autumn 2009, *Asian Cha* Weblog March 2012, *The Prairie Schooner* E-Zine August 2013, *Outloud Too* 2014.

Note from the publisher

David McKirdy's first collection *Accidental Occidental* was published primarily for Hong Kong distribution in hardcover in 2005 with the assistance of a grant from The Hong Kong Arts Development Council. This volume, now out of print, has been been re-issued in an international paperback edition.

David McKirdy's commitment to both his own work and that of his fellow Hong Kong poets led a few years ago to the introduction of Chameleon's Hong Kong poetry publishing project, under his editorial guidance. Other volumes in the *Chameleon Press Hong Kong poetry series* include:

Goldfish by Jennifer Wong (2012)
The Mental Life of Cities by Eddie Tay (2010)
Ghostmasters by Mani Rao (2010)
Snowblind from my protective colouring by Andrew Barker (2009)
Miss Moon's Class by Viki Holmes (2008)
Summer Cicadas by Jennifer Wong (2006)
100 Poems: 1985-2005 by Mani Rao (2006)
Accidental Occidental by David McKirdy (2005)
Poetry Live: An Anthology of Hong Kong Poetry for Teens (2005)
Clearing Ground by Martin Alexander (2004)
Raincheck Renewed by Kavita Jindal (2004)
Food Court by Timothy Kaiser (2003)

CPSIA information can be obtained at www.ICGtesting.com
Printed in the USA
LVOW10s1426030714

392676LV00017B/470/P

9 789881 862389